Beginner's Guide to Growing Marijuana at Home

Step-by-Step Guide to Cannabis Horticulture from Planting to Harvesting Indoor and Outdoor

George Green

Copyrights

Disclaimer and Terms of Use

Effort has been made to ensure that the information in this book is accurate and complete. However, the author and the publisher do not warrant the accuracy of the information, text, and graphics contained within the book due to the rapidly changing nature of science, research, known and unknown facts, and internet. The author and the publisher do not hold any responsibility for errors, omissions, or contrary interpretation of the subject matter herein. This book is presented solely for motivational and informational purposes only.

The recipes provided in this book are for informational purposes only and are not intended to provide dietary advice. A medical practitioner should be consulted before making any changes in diet. Additionally, recipe cooking times may require adjustment depending on age and quality of appliances. Readers are strongly urged to take all precautions to ensure ingredients are fully cooked in order to avoid the dangers of foodborne illnesses. The recipes and suggestions provided in this book are solely the opinion of the author. The author and publisher do not take any responsibility for any consequences that may result due to following the instructions provided in this book.

ISBN: 978-1978207554

Printed in the United States

Contents

Introduction

As people are realizing the various health benefits of cannabis, it is becoming increasingly popular across the world. In fact, it is gradually becoming legal in certain parts of the world, including the United States. Despite being misunderstood as a harmful narcotic, people are steadily realizing that growing marijuana is actually a rewarding and health-promoting horticultural experience. People use cannabis for different reasons. The most common uses are for recreational and/or medicinal purposes.

Growing your own plant can have many positive aspects. You know the source of your marijuana as you are the one cultivating and treating marijuana plant/plants. You don't need to guess what fertilizers are used or its quality. In many ways, planting marijuana for your personal or medicinal use removes the equation of confusion or mistrust. Be in indoor or outdoor, growing marijuana is an immensely rewarding experience. You get to experience the feeling of accomplishment that comes with growing your plant to full maturity.

No matter if it's for a hobby or for personal and medical purposes, if you are planning to grow your own marijuana for the first time, there are many things you need to consider. You don't need to build a marijuana enterprise by growing more plants than you need. Even a few plants is adequate for beginners to start with. Once you gain experience in successfully growing it, you can increase its quantity.

Save Money & Time: Growing marijuana at home is much cheaper than buying it. Also, it is easily accessible to you.

High Quality: You get to decide the strains to grow based on your personal and medicinal requirements. As you're growing it yourself, you know exactly what you're getting. It is now quite common for cannabis to be contaminated. With homegrown cannabis, you would not have to deal with spiked cannabis and adulterated versions. You get the best quality cannabis when you grow it yourself with care.

The process of growing marijuana consists of many important aspects and phases. One needs to understand each and every characteristic and phase to master the art of marijuana growing. This book contains easy-to-understand and easy-to-follow steps to start growing cannabis plants at home and everything you need to know about the plant and its needs. Cultivating your own marijuana is a great way to get constant supply, avoid high prices, and avoid demanding suppliers.

This book provides you with detailed information covering different important aspects and phases including;
- Basic equipment needed including containers, fertilizers, lights
- Selection of seeds, clones & strains
- Planting basics including watering, light, and feeding schedule

- Caring suggestion for marijuana plants for optimum yield
- Flowering and blossoming stage
- Harvesting technique and marijuana curing
- Post harvesting care
- Common mistakes to avoid

Before you start growing plants at home, it is a must for anyone to know about laws related to marijuana cultivation. Refer to official websites of your government to read laws and keep them in mind while you go about growing and using marijuana.

Time Cycle

The marijuana plant does not take long to mature. In most cases, it will take about three months for most strains to be ready for harvesting and curing. Some strain varieties may take less than three months, while others may take longer. Moreover, if you want a large plant/yield, then you will have to wait longer.

Harvesting and Curing

After the harvesting phase is over, you will need to dry it for about six to seven days. It is also advisable to cure the buds in order to produce a more potent and smoother smoke. Without curing, the smoke produced is quite harsh. Curing allows chemicals such as chlorophyll and other sugars to break down. Curing is carried out in an airtight container and takes about 2 to 4 weeks. In a nutshell, it takes about four to six months, between selecting the seeds/clones and the finished product.

When you have decided on your growing method (indoor or outdoor), type of marijuana strain, and growing location, you're good to go, and ready to grow your marijuana plant. Let's embark on this wonderful journey to grow the best possible marijuana at home.

Indoor Marijuana Growing

If you are an indoor gardener now, then you may already possess many of the tools and other requirements needed for growing cannabis. However, if this is your first time, there is no need to worry as all the tools and equipment are easy to source and use.

It is easier and safer to grow marijuana indoors, in an apartment or a house. For indoor planting, cannabis plants grow in the private environment and is safe from prying. You can grow plants throughout a year, and they are safe from animals and insects that can feed on them.

Image: indoor set up for growing cannabis

Just like any other plant, cannabis plants demand sufficient soil, water, and light exposure to flourish. These plants can grow in a smaller space. However, the vertical space required for the plant to grow should be at least 1.5 meters/5 feet. In some cases, even this height will limit your options, but if you ensure this height, you will be able to grow plants with satisfying yield. Your planting space needs an adequate source of ventilation so that heat, moisture, and air can circulate freely. Also, it should be easy to move the plants from time to time.

If you choose to grow cannabis in the closet or a box, make sure to ventilate it by opening the lid or the door at some point during the day. The best place for the plant is a window on the south side of your apartment or house. Putting a plant in front of that window, one can ensure the exposure of natural sunshine. However, with artificial lighting, you can easily replace natural sunshine with lighting lamps. Plants grow under artificial light along with a reflective material so that the plant can get all the possible light that is available.

Basic Planting Aspects & Requirements

Grow Box

Grow boxes are used to regulate the environment to grow cannabis plants. The boxes keep your plants in a greenhouse-like environment and helps in maintaining stable temperature. Grow boxes can be made of cabinets, boxes, PC housings, refrigerators, tents, and more. The possibilities are endless when it comes to grow boxes, and they are only dependent on your imagination. So you can be creative as long as you keep the preferred growing conditions in mind.

The inside of grow boxes is very reflective in order to ensure that your plants get the most light energy. The inside must be coated with a material for an optimum reflection and usage of light:
- White matte color - 80% reflection
- Aluminum foil - 75% reflection
- Black and white foil - 85% reflection
- Mylar foil - 95% reflection

The outsides are usually black or dark-colored and keep the plants warm. They also keep any light from entering the tent to ensure that the plants get their routine cycle of total darkness and total light as you determine.

Image: A Marijuana Grow Tent

You need to decide first about the kind of box you actually require. The size of the space for growing is determined by the area that the lighting will cover. The height is determined by your chosen plant variety. Sativa demands high room, cannabis Indica demands medium room, while Ruderalis demands lower space. The room must have an opening so that fresh air can get in to guarantee an adequate supply of air throughout the cannabis growing cycle.

It is critical to continuously monitor both temperature and humidity levels in the room. Optimal values that your room should have are 27 degrees C temperature, 60% humidity level during vegetation, and 40% humidity level during the process of flourishing.

Lighting Requirement

Light is probably one of the most important aspects for growing healthy marijuana plants. As a tropical plant, marijuana needs a lot of sunlight to grow properly. If you live in more temperate parts of the world, the chances are high that you won't receive enough sunlight for healthy growth. One of the perks of growing marijuana indoors is that you have complete control over its growing, harvesting, and curing process. When you grow marijuana indoors, you need lights that can replace natural sunlight to enable a healthy plant growth. There are a few choices for lighting. It depends on how many plants you want to grow.

High Intensity Discharge (HID) Light/Bulbs
High Intensity Discharge bulbs are the brightest and best choice for your cannabis. In comparison with fluorescent lights, HID bulbs are much more expensive, but they are ideal to grow many more plants.

You have many choices to pick from including Metal Halide, High Pressure Sodium, Low Pressure Sodium, and Mercury Vapor Bulbs. For cannabis gardening, it is best to use HPS (High Pressure Sodium) or MH (Metal Halide) as they are convenient and easy to use. You can use either of the lamps because they both deliver excellent yield. These are lamps that are similar to those used for street lighting.

Image: (MH) Metal Halide Lights

Image: HPS (High Pressure Sodium)

These lamps require a special ballast and ignitor (starter). MH emits white light, and HPS emits orange-violet light that you can see with the lamps for night lighting. HPS lamps emit about 15% to 16% more light than MH lamps. MH and HPS lamps come with a transformer and cost between $150 to $350. They promote fast growth and help in producing larger yields with potent, dense buds.

LED grow lights are another choice for HID bulbs, but they are very expensive. They have been recently introduced in the market and are slowly gaining popularity for marijuana growing. They consume a reasonable amount of electricity and are suitable for growing many plants. LED lights promotes healthier growth and are effective in producing greener, better-looking buds.

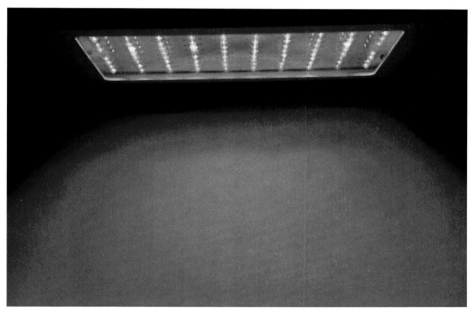

Image: LED Grow Lights

Fluorescent lights

If you wish to grow only a few plants, between 1 to 4 plants, fluorescent lights are a smart choice for you. A single 150-watt CFL (Compact fluorescent light) should be good enough for ideal growth. However, they are also used for growing large number of plants. You just have to increase number of lights based on the number of plants you want to grow. CFL lights broadcast less heat than HID lamps, but considering they give less lumen, they are better for smaller spaces.

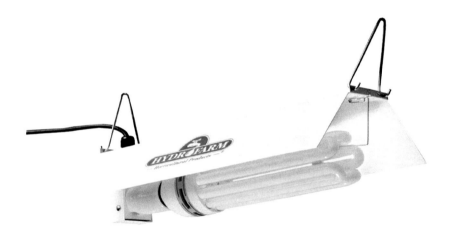

Image: Fluorescent lights

These are made in the form of rods that are interlocked.
Fluorescent lights have certain benefits. They scatter light
throughout the tube so that no part of it is dangerous for the
plant. That means that you can put the plants quite close to
them. They are effective because they emit different colors of
light. Warm white (slightly yellow), cold-white (pure white light),
and daylight correspond to the spectrum and the types of light.

If you use this professional lamp, you will need luminance indicative for an ideal plant growth. Ideal range of luminance is 30W to 50W for MH and HPS lamps. In case of fluorescent tubes, the range is between 40W to 60W. All this refers to one square meter of space.

Basic Planting Tool Set

Pot or Containers

You need containers to grow your plants in. Fabric Pots are very popular. Containers come in different sizes and are made from plastic, metals. and other materials. Make sure that you purchase containers that are flexible and durable so that you can use them again for your next plating phase. It's better to choose containers or pots that have a size of at least one gallon so that there is plenty of area for roots to grow. Containers allow water to drain through effortlessly, and they maintain ideal moisture level. They allow the roots to more easily access oxygen. Availability of oxygen is very critical for an ideal plant cultivation.

Fabric pots are made keeping in mind latest the cultivation techniques. That's why they are also called "smart pots." They prevent cannabis plants from being rootbound and allow growth of new roots.

Properly developed and larger root systems will provide you with bigger yield. Make sure that your chosen containers fit well in the growing box.

Image: Cannabis Plants Grown in Pots/Containers

Timer

This is an optional tool if you find it uncomfortable or difficult to turn the lightning on and off every day. Purchase a digital timer to help you in managing multiple programs.

Thermo/hygrometer

Thermo/hygrometer is an exclusive device for measuring humidity and temperature and is a very critical tool for growing marijuana. Make sure to check temperature level at the top of the plant. Maintain the temperature and humidity levels as much close as possible to respective optimal values. The difference in day/night temperature should not be more than 10 degrees. Low humidity invites insects. Excessive humidity can cause mold during a plant's flowering stage.

pH Meter

A pH meter is one of the most crucial devices for cannabis cultivation. Without a pH meter, there is a high chance of inadequate use of nutrients from the soil, and it can lead to overfeeding and other cultivation issues.

Fertilizers

You can't expect a good yield without providing adequate quality of food to cannabis, so purchase a quality fertilizer for vegetation and flowering.

Eco-Grow and Rapid-Gro are two fertilizers that are popular and quite effective to get for your cannabis plants. However, there are also many other excellent brands out there. There are fertilizers having unique qualities; for instance, there are fertilizers designed exclusively for the growth period. Similarly, you will find fertilizers entirely designed for the flowering period.

Planting Preparations

Selecting & Preparing Soil Mix

Be sure to purchase quality, sterile soil or soil mix containing all the necessities for cannabis to grow and develop. By selecting some of the best of soil types, you can avoid many issues associated with pests and weeds. Some of the quality and popular soil types are: Potgrond Terra Brill, Compo Sana, Terra Magma, and Klasmann. Always purchase your soil type that is suitable for flowering plants. Soil from the garden, and those for orchids, cacti, citrus, palm trees are definitely not suitable to grow cannabis.

You can purchase top-quality soil mix from your local garden center. Marijuana plants need a soil mix that can easily drain water from their containers. A well-draining soil mix consists of sand or some peat moss. Look out for ingredients such as sand sponge rock and pearlite in available choices of soil mixtures. The mix should also contain humus. Most soil mixes are augmented with nutrients with an ideal pH value.

Get to know about the specification of the soil before purchasing. Pick the soil type that is airy so that the root system gets adequate oxygen during the complete growing cycle. Absorption of nutrients by cannabis plants depends on the pH of the soil or soil mixture. Your soil type or soil mixture should have pH value between 6.5 to 7.5. An ideal pH value indicates that you wouldn't need to add any fertilizer to your mix until you reach the flowering stage. It is very critical to check the pH of your soil mix regularly.

You also have an option to create your own potting mix at home. Take 2 parts peat moss and mix it with 1-part sand or perlite. Using a pH meter, you can check the pH of your mix. If the pH is too low, it indicates that your mixture is acidic. In that case, just add lime in the ratio of half a pound of lime to 1 cubic foot of your soil mix.

As far as soil preparation is concerned, breathability of the soil can be achieved by adding soil granules like perlite or Styrofoam. These two granules do not absorb moisture. You can also add some vermiculite, which is a moisture-absorbing granule.

It is critical to make a good drainage to let the full flow of water from the flowerpot. Make sure to place clay beads on the bottom to prevent water from accumulating on the bottom of the container. You can also place them on the soil surface to avoid rapid evaporation of moisture from the soil. This makes for less watering.

Ventilation Management

The area for planting must have good ventilation so that plants can easily consume fresh air. Air intake is usually carried out by a passive inlet vent. Another option is a fan with less capacity that is usually placed in the bottom part of the planting area. PC or bathroom fans are placed to carry out similar functions.

For the air outlet, you need to place a stronger fan (turbine or bathroom fan) in order to generate a negative pressure. It will enable faster air exchange in your area, and as warm air accumulates on the top part, the fan should be placed at the top of the cultivation space.

Apart from fans for air outlet and air intake, you also need an oscillating fan to blow cannabis. The job of an oscillating fan is to imitate natural wind. Your plants will strengthen and will mix the air in the box.

Taking good care of ventilation helps in
- Controlling humidity level of your growing area
- Maintaining ideal room temperature
- Assisting in replenishing carbon dioxide for photosynthesis

Carbon Filters
Installing carbon filters is an option that helps in removing the smell of cannabis from your indoor cultivation area. If the smell bothers you or if you don't want the cannabis smell to leak outside your home, then it's a convenient choice to install it.

Filter System
Filter system is another ventilation solution that can be used instead of an oscillating fan, air intake fan, or an air outlet fan. If you are planning to grow just 1 or 2 plants, then you don't need to worry about ventilation. If you are growing a large number of plants, then you need to set in place a fan filter system for your cannabis.

This fan filter system consists of a fan, a duct, and a filter. You can either purchase it from local garden center, or you can get it at online sources including eBay, Amazon, and other sites. The system is easy to install and comes with instructional manuals. It ensures that your plants remain well aerated. Also the system filters out the scent of the growing cannabis.

Preparing Containers or Pots

First you need to decide on how many containers/vessels you want to put in the box. You need at least 40 cm of area per plant. For example, a box sized 40x40cm can grow 2 plants). Do not place too many containers together as you might end up with too many plants in your planting box.

When you finalize containers and the number of cannabis plants you want to grow, the next thing is to prepare containers for the soil. Take the vessels and make holes in the bottom of the bowl, and place clay beads at the bottom to cover it completely. Now add your chosen soil type or soil mix in the vessels. Gently press the layers of your soil, but not too hard. Pour water, and when the soil settles from watering, add more soil on top.

Making the Right Choice for You

As a beginner, you should decide whether you wish to grow cannabis from seeds or clones. Both options have their merits and demerits. Before planning to grow marijuana, it becomes of the utmost importance to understand the differences of each method and find out what's best for you based on your usage requirements.

Which Is Better? - Cannabis Clones or Cannabis Seeds?

Cannabis Clones

Merits of Using Clones
- With a clone, you can cultivate it into a "mother" and then re-clone it. It provides a steady source of new plants.

- Clones are genetically identical to the "mother." That's why you'll know exactly what you're getting.

- You have an option to "coax" root clones to flower almost immediately, in case space or time is an issue.

- You will get a head start with clones as compared to growing from seed. A clone has a shorter overall growth period. It is also harvest-ready to grow in real quick time.

- With clones, the gender is guaranteed. If the mother plant is female, the clone will also be female.

Demerits of Using Clones

- Clones are harder to source in comparison with seeds because of a lack of qualified cannabis suppliers. Seeds, on the other hand, are almost readily available due to online sources such as seed banks.

- If your clone hasn't been established well, it might die or not grow properly. If grown incorrectly, cloning may take a few extra weeks of care and time for the cannabis plant to recover.

- Newly created clones are more sensitive to light and nutrients when compared with young seed-grown plants.

- If the owner of clones experienced problems like pests or viruses with the "mother" plant, the same problems may happen while growing indoor or outdoor.

In order to purchase marijuana clones, you need to know someone having marijuana plants. You can also purchase from any local medical marijuana dispensary if you are in a suitable location. You can also get a recommendation from your doctor.

Cannabis Seeds

Merits of Using Seeds:

- When you purchase feminized seeds from a seed bank, you can be sure that your plants are 100% female, which are the only ones that form buds.

- When you purchase seeds, you get a "clean slate." It indicates that your plants do not come with pests or disease.

- When you purchase seeds from a reliable seed bank, you'll have a good idea on how your plants will be in terms of quality, flowering time, yield, and looks, provided that you take good care of the plants when growing.

- Mating two plants means you can breed marijuana seeds, which gives you an opportunity to grow unlimited seeds.

- Healthy seeds can be stored in a dark and cool place. You can even store them in your refrigerator (don't ever store in the freezer) until you are ready to use them.

Demerits of Using Clones:

- Breeding your own seeds may save you money. However, you still need to invest a lot of time and effort in mating two plants.

- Not all seeds will germinate.

- If you buy seeds every time you grow, it may turn out to be a costly affair. Also, many popular cannabis strains may be more expensive per seed.

- Seeds take longer to grow and mature than clones. Cannabis clones are already established and "mature" when you start growing them.

- If you don't purchase feminized seeds, around 50% of your plants may grow to be male.

- Old or Improperly-stored seeds may grow more slowly.

When using seeds, you need to decide on your plants' gender. Healthy seeds are either light gray or dark brown. If the seeds are small and white, they may be immature and won't properly germinate.

Properly stored seeds are still viable after a few years, although it may prolong germination time and you may get more duds as compared to fresh seeds. Cannabis seedlings from older seeds may also grow more slowly.

Selecting the Right Strain for Your Needs

A particular strain of cannabis can help in the therapy of many specific medical symptoms. For an instance, to reduce anxiety, some of the most effective strains to handle such symptom are LA Confidential, Romulan, Mazar, or Northern Light. For pain management, you may want to grow Blue Dream, Sour Diesel, Romulan, Jack Herer, LA Confidential, or Grape Ape.

When you grow cannabis, either from seeds or clones, choose a strain that fits your custom requirements such as treating symptoms like anxiety, pain, or nausea. Different strains have different compatibilities. You need to consider a certain types of strain that can match up with your growing method, expected growing time, and growing conditions.

Common Cannabis Varieties

Before you buy cannabis clones or seeds, you need to know some of the main things about marijuana strains. Each strain has their own unique profile and growing needs, and they all have varying effects on individuals.

Sativa
Sativa grows tall and lanky with fingerlike, thin leaves. Sativa buds are less dense and more airy when compared to Indica buds, and they normally have a longer flowering period. They are best suited for growing marijuana outdoor as they can grow as much as 20 feet in height. However, one can grow Sativa indoors also, as it is possible to control its shape and height.

Sativa strains have relieving effects on migraines, depression, and certain kinds of pain. Sativa buds are sometimes psychedelic, energizing and uplift the mood.

Haze
Haze is considered as a Sativa-dominant variety. Its plant has special properties. The strain's genetics are a combination of many varieties of Sativa plants from Thailand, Colombia, India, and Mexico. Haze plants have psychedelic and mood-uplifting effects. Moreover, they have endowed genetic traits to cannabis strains such as Jack Herer, Northern Light, and Super Lemon Haze. Apart from being shorter than Sativa and having long flowering periods, they are far easier to grow in an indoor setting than a full Sativa.

Indica
Indica plant resembles a Christmas tree, tends to grow short and bushy with wide leaves. Their buds tend to deliver a heavier and relaxing effect. They are best suited for indoor cultivation due to their shape. Indica strains tend to deliver relieving effects in case of muscle tension, lack of appetite, nausea, insomnia, body pain, depression, and anxiety.

Ruderalis
A Ruderalis plant goes through a 3-month lifecycle, regardless of how you maintain it. The Ruderalis flowers grow on their own naturally. This cannabis strain may have no psychoactive properties of their own, but its pure plants have been genetically combined with other strains for one unique property. If you like to harvest Ruderalis in a large quantity, it can be an issue. Their plants tend to be short and are best suited for small, indoor growing. A Ruderalis plant contains lesser concentrations of tetrahydrocannabinol (THC) as compared to other cannabis strains. Ruderalis strains tend to have higher cannabidiol (CBD) levels, and have many medical purposes, including anxiety management.

Popular Cannabis Strains for Beginners

AK-48
AK-48 is a hybrid of Jock Horror and Ice (Shiva, Skunk, Afghan, and Northern Lights). They are relatively easy to grow and assist in relieving anxiety and stress for many users. It grows both outdoors and indoors, in soil and in hydro. Apart from being resistant to root problems, AK-48 reacts well to growth control techniques. Their strains, however, do not grow well in temperatures above 30°C (85°F). With an above-average yield, the pleasantly sweet and strong odor intensifies towards the terminal phase of its flowering stage, close to harvest time.

Aurora Indica
This particular cannabis strain is a hybrid of Northern Lights and Afghan. Its medicinal use includes nausea treatment. It can thrive even in higher temperatures. After a 7-9 week long flowering period, Aurora Indica gets ready for harvesting. Its odor becomes heavy close to harvest time. It is high-yielding and has ample-sized bud sites.

Super Lemon Haze
This cannabis stain demands 2½ to 3½ months for its flowering stage. The plant can grow tall and resembles a Christmas tree. With the combined genetics of the Super Silver Haze and Lemon Skunk strains, this unique strain delivers high yields.

Jack Herer
With a medium to tall height, this cannabis strain's genetics are unknown, but are believed to be either Sativa, Haze, or Indica. For medical uses, it provides relief from muscle spasms, headaches, and pain. Moreover, it is used to relieve anxiety or stress. Jack Herer can at least double in height after its flowering stage completes unless growth control methods are used to restrict its height. You can harvest this strain for around 2

½months into flowering. Jack Herer is best grown indoors but can be grown outside in a sunny climate. The yield of the strain is average.

Northern Light
Possibly derived from Indica, Northern Light is used for relaxation or stress relief. The short and hardy strain is usually ready for harvest after two months of flowering. The dense buds normally don't emit a strong odor. It also reacts well to growth control techniques like low-stress training. The Northern Light strain is best for stealth and/or indoor growing, though other people report of having successfully growing it outdoors. The yields are average or above average.

Sprouting & Sowing Seeds

After selecting your suitable marijuana strain, you need to learn how to germinate and then sow them to begin their growing journey.

When planting the seeds, you do not necessarily need to know the characteristics of plants as well as gender. If you are going to purchase your seeds from a seed bank, you can choose between regular seeds (a certain percentage of male plants) or feminized seeds (99% female plants). In both cases, characteristics of your chosen variety are known. It is important to know that you can use only female plants. Male cannabis plants are not welcome in the pits due to pollination. Male plants are utilized purposefully in the target-pollination to obtain seeds.

Sprouting/Germinating the Seeds

You have two options to germinate the seeds:

1) Using a handkerchief method.
Take a handkerchief and wet it with cold running water. Place the seeds in it, and coat with another handkerchief. Moisten both the handkerchiefs with water. Keep them in a dark, warm place. It will help in sprouting the seeds.

Another option is to place the seeds in a glass of water (adjusted PH) instead of using handkerchiefs. Keep them in water for 24-48 hours. Soon they will begin to sprout.

2.) Using Starter Plugs

For the purpose of sprouting, another convenient way is to use starter plugs or cubes. They guarantee a very high germination rate. Starter plugs are suitable to germinate all kinds of plants. They are easily available at your local garden center, a mall, or online stores.

Sowing

When the seeds start germinating, place them in the prepared pots (one seed per pot), and cover with 2-3 mm of soil. Place your selected source of light over the seedlings, about 5 or 6 inches above the seed area.

One important thing to remember is to make sure that the lights are always on. Continuous light exposure accelerates the growth of your plants. After the seedlings sprout their first 2 leaves, officially they are not seedlings as they have now entered the critical stage of vegetation.

Initial Growing Stage

Your cannabis seeds have germinated, meaning they have entered the vegetative stage. This is an important stage in the plant's life as this is when they start growing and gradually progressing towards the flowering stage. The growing stage is like when a child hits puberty. During initial growing stage, you need to take care of your plants' water, food, light, and temperature requirement for their healthy growth and optimum yield.

Initial growing stage

Feeding Requirements

When feeding cannabis plants, it is important to know about the nutrients that your soil or soil mixture already has. Depending on your fertilizer type, simply follow the instructions about the timings and number of times to feed the plants. When you start feeding, supply your plants with a half-strength fertilizer. After the plants start growing vigorously, you can increase the fertilizer to 3/4th strength. If your leaves begin to appear yellowish, then your plants aren't getting enough nutrients. If you have followed your fertilizer's feeding instructions properly, and still your plants aren't getting enough nutrients, then it is time to re-check the pH level of your soil mix. The pH level must fall under the range mentioned earlier.

Lighting Requirements

During the vegetative periods, your plants need maximum light exposure. About 18 to 23 hours a day of light is what cannabis plants need for healthy growth. As long as you provide your plants with a lot of light and very few dark hours (between 1 to 6 hours, depending on the strain), they will remain in the vegetative stage. Auto flowering strains are an exception to this rule.

Lighting requirements during the vegetative stage is between a ratio of 18/6 (18 hours of light exposure, 6 hours of complete darkness) to 24-0 (24 hours of light exposure, 0 dark hour). After cannabis plants have grown to your satisfaction, they will enter the flowering stage in which they will need a 12-12 schedule. This is when you give the plant 12 hours of light and 12 hours of complete darkness (covered in upcoming chapters). If you want cannabis plants to grow small then you can start with a 12-12 schedule right from the seeds sowing.

Temperature Requirements

The marijuana plant is a tropical plant, and it grows best in warmth. In its natural homes, temperature level is usually around 30+°C /90+° F. However, that doesn't mean that you need to provide such a high temperature level to cannabis for indoor growing. Marijuana plants grow just fine in the average room temperatures between 20-30° C (70 to 85° F). As far as the temperature is not freezing, your plants will grow in a safe, temperate level.

Watering Requirements

You should ensure that your cannabis plants are well-watered, but not under-watered or overwatered. Only provide water to your plants when the top part of your soil mix is dry. You can determine it when the soil separates from the edge of the container/pot. It is time to water the plant when they hang a bit. It shows that they are thirsty.

As a beginner, a simple way to find out if your soil mix needs watering is to stick your finger into the mix just until the first knuckle, if it feels dry, then it is time to water.

However, if you water your plants too often, it will drown their roots and kill the plant. When watering your plant, make sure you water the complete soil area (not just one spot) until water runs down the bottom of your container. Make sure your containers/pots are well drained and supply water again when the topsoil feels dry.

Plants Symptoms during excessive water supply
- Firm leaves; curled up all the way to the stem
- Yellowish leaf appearance
- Drooping leaves

Plants Symptoms during less water supply
- Lifeless, limp leaves that may be dry and crispy
- Wilting leaves
- In extreme case, death of plant

Be sure to measure the pH value of the water you are pouring in the pots. You can measure pH by using a pH meter. The plant can absorb nutrients only in a certain range of pH level, so be sure to check the pH value.

If you are supplying the tap water, leave it aside in a separate container for a day or two so that all the chlorine evaporates from the water, and then pour it into the pots. If your water's pH level is higher than 6.5-7, you can lower the pH value by adding lemon juice, citric acid, or vinegar. Also sodium bicarbonate and some of the finished products help in increasing the pH value.

It would not be a bad idea to ventilate the water. You can use an air pump, i.e. put the air stone into the water, and connect it with the silicone hose. Exhausting the air through the pump, the water will get enriched with oxygen.

Pests
Pests are some of the things for which you have to be watchful when growing marijuana indoors. Know the infestation signs and eradicate them before it's too late as they can fully ruin your crop. Some of the common signs are white spots on leaves, a moldy odor, or black spots on leaves. Look closely at the plant's leaves to see if anything is off. Use garlic spray regularly as it's an effective preventative procedure that makes your marijuana plants repulsive to pests.

Train Your Cannabis for Optimum Yield

Before your plant reaches the flowering stage, you need to consider a few ways to train your cannabis plants to grow short but bushy. Training your cannabis plant is not compulsory. Cannabis training is more required when you have less space and want to maximize yield. Without training your plants, you will get adequate yield after harvesting so it is purely an option for all cannabis growers.

There are primarily two methods for cannabis training:
1) **Low Stress Training**
2) **Defoliation**

Low Stress Training

This one of the smart options to train your plants and control their growth without harming them. For low stress training, you will need a few supplies.
- A plant in the vegetative stage
- Scissors or pruners
- Some Plant twisty ties (Easily available at your nearest garden center or online stores)

Bend Down Technique
Bending your plants is very effective technique to keep cannabis plant low and increase their yield. The purpose is to ensure that the whole plant get better access to light.
- You can simply bend down the main stem, like a magnet is attracting the plant from the other side. Do it gently to avoid breaking the stem.
  You can also bend down all the stems outwards. it will resemble a star-like shape.

There are many techniques in which you can bend the cannabis stems. After you have bent the main stem or all the stems down, use plant twisty ties to keep them in place. Soft wire ties can be used for big tall cannabis plants.

- The most used technique is to secure them into place.
- Drilling holes in the pots or containers and then fastening the ties to the holes.
- If you're using fabric pots, you can use safety pins to pierce them and fasten the ties to the pins.
- You can fasten the ties to fishing weights so that gravity can assist in pulling them down as they hang.

The purpose is to hold down your branches so that the plants get maximum airflow and light exposure. You can be creative and tie down the stems in your intended way as long as it fulfill the purpose.

Bend down growing cannabis plants – string used to bend down the plant

Topping Technique

When your plant has grown about 5 to 7 nodes, then you can start topping the plant. The topping technique includes cutting/pruning the top of the plant. It is advisable to top your plants to the 3rd node. Each level of leaves is 1 node. This means that, you will cut of your plant at the 3rd node.

Care should be taken not to prune or cut off the auxiliary shoots. You should also leave a little bit of stem when you top off.

Important Tips to Remember:
- Train the plants when they are young. Do it before the soft stem grows and become a thick, hard one.
- If you begin training them at a young age before they develop thick stems, you will only need to bend new growth and it will make your job much easier.
- Only bend soft flexible stems to prevent breakage.
- Be gentle when you bend the stems. You don't want to break the stem.
- Make sure that the ties are securely attached to plants. Your ties should be secure, but not scraping or moving along the stem as it can damage the plant.
- Use several ties attached to different parts of the stems in order to hold stubborn stems down.

Defoliation Technique

This is the training technique of removing the leaves of vigorously growing cannabis plants. The purpose is to mean the branches/colas (the terminal bud), which you have defoliated to grow much more slowly. Defoliation prevents the tress from growing too tall and developing a Christmas tree shape. A Christmas tree shape will cause the buds on lower branches to not get enough light, and it will hamper the overall cannabis yield. After your trees start budding, do not remove the tiny shoots.

When defoliating, you can remove the colas/branches that you feel have grown excessively. It is advised not to remove more than 50% of the plant's vegetation at a single time. The best time to defoliate is in the vegetative stage. After you defoliate the plants, allow them to grow back the foliage lost.

Flowering: Terminal Growing Stage

Flowering is the last stage of your growing season. After the flowering stage, you will be harvesting and curing your cannabis. Many requirements including lighting schedule change during this important phase.

The New Lighting Schedule

When to switch to the flowering stage is solely your decision as its right time is associated with your expectations and yield requirement. When you feel your plant has grown enough, then you can switch over to the flowering stage. Remember the larger your plant, the more yield it will give. In most cases, cannabis growers keep the plants in the vegetative stage for about a month. However, 2 ½ weeks of time is also adequate to switch to the flowering stage.

During the flowering stage, maintain the light schedule to a 12-12 schedule; provide your plants with 12 hours of light, then 12 hours of complete darkness. This new light schedule is similar to if you're growing your plants outdoors. After you switch your plants to the flowering stage, they will be ready to harvest in about 2 ½ months.

Once you switch to a 12-12 light schedule, the plants will take about 3 weeks to reach the flowering stage. During the flowering stage, the size of your plants will double or triple. You can continue training your plants during the flowering stage. You can use the Low Stress Technique to bend down branches that have grown too tall. This technique will ensure that all parts of your cannabis plants get the same amount of light exposure.

Male & Female Cannabis

During the flowering stage, you need to find out the gender of your plants. As a grower, only female plants are important to you as those are the ones that produce the buds. Male plants grow pollen sacs. If you don't pluck out the male plants, they will fertilize the female plants. The fertilization process drops the levels of THC and cannabinoids dramatically in female plants, and the plants will produce seeds instead of buds, damaging overall yield.

It seems like a daunting task to be watchful about the male plants. However, all it needs is a close daily inspection. The gender signs normally appear about 1 to 3 weeks after you have switched to the new 12-12 light schedule. Male plants will produce pollen sacs (resembling tiny balls), while the female plants will produce pistils (resembling white hairs). However, care has to be taken to not confuse sturdy green growths with pistils. Both males and female produce green growths.

Female cannabis plant

Male cannabis plant

Now that you know what to look out for, you can get rid of all male plants. Remove all male plants as soon as their pollen sacs appear. If you have kept your plants in the vegetative stage for long enough, some strains may produce pre-flowers.

New Requirements

In the flowering stage, your cannabis plants are most susceptible to pH levels and your soil mixture's nutritional level. Do not forget to test for pH levels regularly and closely follow the feeding instructions that came with your chosen fertilizer. After the first two months of flowering, it is not advisable to up the amount of nutrients to feed your plants. Many cannabis growers give their plants only water getting during the last few weeks of the flowering stage. The leaves will begin to die and the buds will keep on ripening. This isn't a sign that your plant needs more nutrients; it is just the natural aging process. Ensure to maintain the temperature level between 65 and 80° F (18 and 26° C). 65° F or 18° C during the night and 80° F or 26° C during the day.

Soil Flushing

About 10 days before the harvesting phase, it is required to flush the soil with plenty of water (about 5 times greater than the volume of the container). The washout is also desirable during overfeeding, as it helps to flush toxic salts that accumulate on the roots. Due to flushing, all the fertilizers gathered in the soil will be washed out. In the last few days, cannabis plants will draw nutrients from the last reserves in the leaves and the leaves will start turning yellowish just like the autumn.

Water the plants with pure water, and add a little honey or sugar cane molasses when watering for the last time. During the last 24-48 hours, it is advised to keep the plant in the dark. According to some researches, secretion of THC is then increased, but more likely this is because of the decomposition of chlorophyll.

Harvesting Cannabis and Curing

The main concern here is when to harvest your plants and how to determine the right time for harvesting. To determine the right time, you need to keep in mind the following points:

- As your plants move towards the end of life, the buds will stop growing white hairs on them. The plants will become highly fragrant.

- Wait until about 40 percent of the buds darken in color and start curling up. At this point, you can start harvesting your plants. However, the plants have not reach their full potency by that time. Using such buds after drying or curing can make some users anxious and also give some headaches.

- When about 50% to 70% of the hairs darken, it means that THC levels in your plants are at its maximum level. This is the time you can harvest your buds.

- You can also wait until 80 to 90% of the hairs darken. Using such buds, after drying or curing, give users a relaxed feeling. Users get such a relaxing effect because some of the THC has been converted to the more relaxing CBN (Cannabinol).

Another way to determine the right time is to inspect the buds under a jeweler's magnifying glass. You will see tiny droplets that look like water dew drops. These are normally clear in appearance during their flowering stage. When they appear milky, the time is good to harvest them.

Materials Required

1) String and nails: You may also use a drying rack; it depends on your harvest size.

2) Clippers: You can use pruning shears, scissors, or a sharp garden knife.

3) Paper bags

4) Large size canning jars

How to Harvest:
Starting with the stem, cut off the main branches of your plants. Cut as big as you can. Your cutting depends on the space you have for the next step of drying. If you don't have a large space, cut the branches into smaller pieces.

You may cut the leaves off, or you can keep them as is. You can let the leaves remain on the branches as you dry the buds. You can use a tumbler to pluck the leaves the moment they are fully dried.

Drying Cannabis Buds

You are almost done preparing marijuana for medicinal or personal use. You can start using your buds right after drying them. Another option is to cure them for the best taste, smell, and smoothness.

In order to dry your buds, trim them first. When you cut down all the peaks along with the part of the stem, it is time to cut off all the leaves, and trim the leaves that are close to the peaks.

You can also decide to trim after drying. The drying process is very simple. Just take the buds, make a series of flower peaks on the rope and hang them upside-down in a cool, dry, dark place. Make sure that the area is well-ventilated. Dry your buds slowly and in a natural way. After a few days of drying (depending on the humidity level and room temperature), peaks will become completely dry. Ensure that tops of the flowers are not touching each other. Inspect them regularly to look out for mold and signs for over drying.

Image: Drying Cannabis

You can also dry them in a well-ventilated box, making sure that the tops do not directly touch the fan. You will recognize dried peaks as the stems will become easy to break.

Curing Cannabis

If you want to smoke your marijuana for medicinal purposes, you can opt to cure the buds. After your buds have dried up completely, when you can easily snap thin stems but thick stems are still a little flexible), it's time to cure the buds.

The process of curing is very easy.
- A few days after harvesting, you buds will develop a crispy texture. At this time, put them in paper bags, which should be kept open.
- Shake them several times a day; it will ensure dryness. Do it for the next 2-3 days.
- Take mason jars and fill them about 70% with the dried buds. Close them tightly with top lid.
- For the next 14 days, open the jars daily for a few seconds, and then close again.
- If you feel any sign of moisture, keep the jar open so that the buds can dry out.
- After 14 days, you can open the jars after every 5 to 7 days for a few seconds (provided there is no sign of moisture.

Most people cure their cannabis for 2-3 weeks, while others cure them for 1-2 months. You can stop curing your harvest if you feel they have been cured enough. About 30-35 days of curing should be enough. You should then store the cured buds in cool, dry, airtight containers for long term storage and usage. If you get a moldy smell from the jars, get rid of the crop.

Curing requires a lot of attention or your yield could get ruined. After the curing process is complete, your buds should smell like a pleasant Christmas. Your cannabis buds are now ready to use for medicinal or personal usage. You can use them for smoking or you can process the cured buds to prepare cannabutter, cannaoil, tincture, or liniment.

Outdoor Cannabis Growing

Just like indoor growing, outdoor marijuana growing is an easy-to-follow technique with an impressive yield. There are some advantages when you grow marijuana outside, like you don't need to deal with lighting costs since sunlight is absolutely free and a natural way to provide light exposure. When you grow your plant outdoors, all parts of the cannabis plant grow evenly. However, growing outdoors does have its disadvantages too. You need to be precautious about fungi and pests that can kill your crops, and you may have to deal with animals like rodents, chipmunks, and deer that can ruin the plants.

Growing cannabis outside is a great option if your balcony or plot of land is getting adequate sunlight. Pick a non-shady spot, and you are good to go. Visit your plant as often as possible, and be sure that it is properly watered. Exposure to light is vital when deciding a site for an outdoor plot. Choose a location where your plants can get sunlight for maximum hours.

If you are planting directly in the ground, make sure your soil is dark, loamy, and fertile. If you have substandard soil, then give it a treatment with composted manure for at least a season before you start planting cannabis. Ensure that your soil drains well every time you water them. The roots have to dry out fully.

Outdoor grown cannabis will obviously yield more than an indoor setting of cannabis because outside, the plants grow larger. Only a few indoor setups can provide the ability to accommodate plants bigger than 170-180 centimeters/5.5 to 6 feet in height. Outdoor grown plants can grown about 2-3 meters/7-10 feet in height.

You can also grow in your balcony, backyard, or outdoor porch using containers or pots. Choose to purchase pots that are at least a gallon so that there is plenty of area for roots to grow. You can prepare the soil mixture to put in the pots and plant the cannabis using the same steps mentioned earlier for indoor growing.

Image: Outdoor Growing In Pots

Growing Outdoor Checklist

1) Marijuana Clones or Seeds

2) A 4-in-1 measurement tool will be of great use if you want to get the soil's moisture level, soil pH, temperature, and sunlight intensity. It can also help you determine if you need more fertilizer or change your fertilizer type. The tool also helps to check if your soil is draining properly.

3) Fertilizer: You can prepare your own compost tea or compost, or you can buy ready-made fertilizer. Purchase a quality fertilizer for vegetation and flowering. You will find many popular brands based on your locality.

4) Protection: You may need to form a fence around your area of cultivation to protect the plants from gophers, deer, or other hungry animals. However, it depends on your area. If you feel your plants are safe from animals then there is no need to create a fence.

5) Water: A natural water source including a well is the best option. Try not to use the fluoridated municipal water supply or chemically-treated water as such chemicals may end up in your marijuana buds. You can use a drip irrigation system, or you can always use the best method of manual water supply for accuracy and convenience.

Outdoor Growing Challenges

If the buds will have to face heavy rain, wind, or violent storms, it can shred your buds to pieces. Bugs can inhabit them too as they are not protected by indoor growing boxes. Unless it is all about the weed's aroma, it's best to grow marijuana indoors than outdoors. However, if the weed's flavor is of utmost importance, outdoor-grown marijuana is best. One primary concern is the law pertaining to your local government for growing marijuana. If it is prohibited to grow marijuana in your state or country, then outdoor growing is not a smart choice.

Sunlight Exposure

Cannabis are sun-loving plants. The perfect time to plant your marijuana clones depends on your geographical location. When growing weed, temperature requirements along with sunlight exposure are very important.

The best time to plant is in April or May. If you are living in a warmer climate, you can plant in April. If you can plant cannabis as early as possible while the spring season is on, you can ensure maximum sunlight to the plants. Middle of a growing season is a suitable time to provide adequate sunlight exposure. You can even plant cannabis in colder climates as long as the plants are exposed to adequate sunlight. It's critical not to allow the plant to go into the stage of flowering too soon. Your climate conditions should be ideal to allow the plants to become big before they start producing buds.

In order to keep the plants in a vegetative growth stage, exposure of a minimum of 12 hours a day of sunlight is necessary. More is good. If the plants get sunlight for less than 12 hours a day, they will prematurely go into the flowering stage because darkness triggers flowering in plants. More than 12 hours of darkness during a vegetative stage can affect the growth and overall yield.

Growing In Winter

You can also grow marijuana during the winter. Find a suitable land area that is exposed to the winter sun. It's better if the cannabis plants get sunlight from 8 am to 5 pm, but the hours from 10 am to 4 pm also ensure a healthy growth. However, it is more challenging to grow marijuana if you live in latitudes north of 30° since the days are shorter.

During the winter, a hill's south side normally gets the most sun. Large open land space to a property's northern side is likely to get excellent sun exposures. West and east side land space may be good if they get the full morning, mid-day, and full afternoon sun exposure.

Soil Preparation & Seed Planting

The perfect soil is ideally dark brown in color. It should compact if you squeeze it in palm but break apart easily with a small amount of pressure. You can check the pH level of your possible soil area. An ideal pH level for outdoor growing is between 6 to 6.5.

Image: A Dark Brown Soil

Get rid of any weeds that are already in your chosen growing area. To ensure the little devils do not sprout again, pull them from their roots. You can now mix fertilizers with the soil and use them in different growing stages as per the instructions that came with the fertilizer brand.

Beginners are often faced with the dilemma of which technique to use – seed or clone. For first-time growers, seed planting is a hassle-free technique with fewer difficulties than using clones. For indoor growing, both seeds and clones are equally effective options. However, when it comes to outdoor growing, clones can be tricky for beginners. A seed-grown plant will have a root structure that is hearty and stable for outdoor growing.

For outside cannabis growing, you have two choices: sow the seeds directly on the site, or germinate them at home and then plant them out. The decision is yours as both choices have their benefits. For example, germinating the cannabis seeds at home gives you control over the early stages that are often delicate, while directly planting them prevents damage caused when transporting and transplanting them.

You can germinate the seeds using the same methods of mentioned in the earlier chapter: 1) Using Starter Plugs or 2) Using a handkerchief. For sowing the seeds in the prepared soil, make small holes, maintaining ideal distance between each hole to provide enough space to the plants when they grow. Now place the germinated seeds in the holes and cover with 2-3 mm of a soil layer.

Water Supply

After ensuring adequate sunlight exposure, water is the next most important factor, whether you have decided to grow cannabis in the wild or away from the house. Water supply should be close to the ground surface or be easily accessible. Otherwise, you may need to arrange for a storage solution to properly hydrate your plant. It can be a challenging task as water is quite heavy. Choosing an area near a stream or river should be a smart idea. However, remember that streams and rivers can flood during autumn or spring. Avoid a grow area that has patches of still water because cannabis plants do not like being waterlogged.

If possible, try to look for a land area near a feasible water source. You'll also have to keep a bucket handy to cart the water to your plot. You can use a drip irrigation system with auto timing to water the plants. A much simpler solution is to purchase a five-gallon can, punch several small holes in it, and manually water the plants.

You are watering the plants perfectly if they are growing at least 1 inch a week. If it does, you do not need to supply more water or check for a pH level. Try to use water with a pH of 7. The plant symptoms for under-watering or overwatering are the same as mentioned earlier for indoor growing.

Water your plants well, but don't overwater them. Overwatering can lead to root drowning. The roots must be completely dry prior to watering again. A way to check if your plant is getting too little or too much water is to examine the leaves. Their spikes must turn in the direction of the sun. If the leaves are drooping or are completely flat, re-examine the frequency of your watering.

Cultivating and Harvesting

Just like indoor growing, your plants will first go through a vegetative stage and then the flowering stage. Once they reach the end of the flowering stage, start harvesting the buds using the same technique and precautions mentioned earlier. Now you can dry them at home and then cure them to be used for personal or medical purposes.

Precautions & Common Mistakes to Avoid

If you are growing cannabis for the first time, it is common to worry about making mistakes and blunders. There's a learning curve in every endeavor, and growing marijuana is no different. In growing marijuana, know some of the mistakes that experienced cultivators have committed in their first attempt. Even if you end up making following those mistakes or face unexpected challenges, you will gradually learn how to avoid them all together.

Be Prepared

When you grow marijuana, you may face unexpected situations that can overwhelm you. You should consider the plants' needs like nutrients, carbon dioxide, water, and light. You should also be prepared for other possible challenges like lack of nutrient quality, bug infestations, and insufficient carbon dioxide. Have a contingency plan in case your plants manifest negative signs.

The Pest Challenge

Sometimes unwanted tenants like red spider, fruit flies, fungus gnats, symphilids, thrips, and leaf miners will attack your plant leaves and also their roots. As a precaution, you can use preventive agents such as Neem, a natural pesticide, which effectively protects plants from parasites and microorganisms. It can be added to your soil type, or you can spray it directly on the plants. You can use hydrogen peroxide or put some ladybugs in growing tent, which is a natural predator.

Fruit Flies (Fungus Gnats)

Adult flies lay their eggs on the surface of the soil from which they collect larvae. The larvae feed on roots and organic matter. As a natural solution, place slices of potato that collect larvae on the surface of the soil. After they are gathered, discard the slices. You can also cover the surface of the soil with sand in order to suffocate larvae. The Neem and tobacco extract are also effective remedies to control the larvae issue.

Thrips

Thrips are tiny in appearance but can be seen with the naked eye. They reproduce quickly, and some species are more resistant to chemicals. They suck the juice from the leaves, and it make the leaves appear white. As a solution you can use Neem and ladybugs to control their damaging effects.

Red Spider (Spider Mites)

Red spiders are very challenging to manage and control their harmful effects. They suck juices from the leaves, leaving white spots where they feed. The tobacco extract and Neem are effective remedies against spiders.

Symphilid

Symphilids are light or white-colored and look like caterpillars. They dig the soil surface and feed on roots. When watering, it is easy to observe them as they rise to the surface. Neem and hydrogen peroxide are effective remedies against symphilids.

Leaf Miners

Leaf Miners eat leaves and dig trenches in order to lay their larvae. They form carved lines on the leaves. Neem is an effective agent to control them.

Miscellaneous Problems

Heat Stress

Look at the image below and you will see brownish edges on the leaves and curled-up leaves that indicate heat damage stress in indoor growing. Also for outdoor growing, it indicates a feeding problem. In an indoor-growing setting, these are leaves from the top of the plant. They were closest to the indoor lighting source, and heat damaged them. The only solution is to increase the distance between plants and lamps.

Excessive Watering

If you are supplying the water that has no adjusted pH value, it is possible to disrupt the proper intake of nutrients from the soil, which can hamper a plant's growth. Therefore, nourish it regularly with the set pH value, adhering to the prescribed dose of your chosen fertilizer brand.

Unstable pH

When the pH of your soil is too high or too low, it can block nutrients in the form of salts and compounds and it can be toxic for the plant. It mainly happens when the manufacturer tries to boost consumption of their plant fertilizer, which makes it worse. PH value drops even more and blocks further consumption of nutrients. If the plants start showing any signs of overfeeding, you should stop the food supply, measure the pH value, adjust it within the ideal range, and then start feeding again.

Fertilizer Issue

If you're a beginner, don't just grab any fertilizer. Even if your marijuana plants grow, they won't thrive the way you intend them to. Most trusted fertilizers have an NPK ratio displayed conveniently on the packaging. NPK ration indicates the combination of N (nitrogen), P (phosphorus), and K (potassium) as these three plays a vital role in a healthy growth of your plants.

For each period of growth, excluding the flowering period, you may want to utilize a fertilizer that has a high nitrogen ratio. When your plants are in the flowering stage, you should use a fertilizer with a high phosphorus ration.

Know the Soil

Many beginners may think that any outdoor soil has enough nutrients for their plants. That soil, unfortunately, may not be the soil to produce a healthy plant. That soil may be too alkaline or too acidic. It may not even help to properly germinate your seeds. When you grow marijuana outdoors, be sure to infuse your soil with a soil mix or fertilizer.

Don't Over-prune

Pruning your plants does encourage growth, and you may have heard that more pruning means more growth. However, you don't have to prune your cannabis plants in their entirety. You may only weaken it or even kill the plants if you prune them too much.

Being Active

Growing cannabis demands much of your time. You need to care for them just like your child and need to be patient during their growing phase. Marijuana plants have a short lifespan from fertilization to harvest. It's not a process where you can just plant them and leave them alone. Make sure your plants are getting adequate ventilation, CO_2, and light. Feed them, prune them, trim them, and water them as per your routine schedule.

Conclusion

Growing marijuana is an immensely rewarding and exciting experience. It provides a sense of accomplishment. This book is a complete guide that equips you with all the knowledge you need to grow cannabis indoor as well as outdoors. Whether you are growing for your own smoking pleasure or for medicinal use, following the steps and strategies covered in the book will help you to be able to produce the best quality marijuana at home.

We would like to extend our heartiest gratitude to all the readers to give their precious time in reading this dedicated book on marijuana growing. We hope this book was able to help you in learning step-by-step approach to grow marijuana both indoors and outdoors.

References

http://www.growweedeasy.com/cannabis-grow-lights

https://www.zativo.com/cannabis-grow-guide/seedling-stage

https://www.cannabis.info/en/seedlings

http://www.growweedeasy.com/germinate

https://sensiseeds.com/en/info/faq/best-way-to-germinate-seeds/

http://www.growweedeasy.com/light-schedules

http://www.growweedeasy.com/12-12-from-seed-force-flower

https://www.royalqueenseeds.com/blog-the-different-types-of-lights-for-cannabis-pros-and-cons-n276

http://www.greencultured.co/hps-lighting-for-cannabis-plants/

http://howtogrowmarijuana.com/hps-grow-lights/

http://www.growweedeasy.com/mh-hps-upgrade-guide

http://www.growweedeasy.com/led-grow-lights

http://aquariuscannabis.com/best-ph-balance-grow-marijuana

https://www.theweedblog.com/what-is-the-best-ph-level-for-marijuana-plants/

https://www.royalqueenseeds.com/blog-top-3-ruderalis-indica-strains-n381

http://bigbudsmag.com/the-5-best-strains-for-br-growing-monster-marijuana-plants/

http://www.thenorthwestleaf.com/pages/articles/post/seeds-vs-clones

http://www.dopemagazine.com/clones-or-seeds/

http://growingmarijuanatips.com/tools-that-every-marijuana-grower-should-use/

https://www.how-to-marijuana.com/marijuana-grow-equipment.html

http://growace.com/blog/the-marijuana-checklist-9-things-to-look-for-before-you-buy-your-grow-equipment/

http://www.marijuanapropagation.com/choosing-the-best-marijuana-grow-equipment.html

https://www.royalqueenseeds.com/blog-what-do-you-need-to-start-growing-weed-n121
https://www.theweedblog.com/the-best-soil-growing-marijuana/
http://grow-marijuana.com/medium
https://www.royalqueenseeds.com/blog-create-your-own-soil-mix-for-cannabis-n75
http://www.yates.com.au/gardening/tips/choosing-the-right-potting-mix
https://smartpots.com/which-potting-mix-is-right-for-you/
https://www.alchimiaweb.com/blogen/ventilation-marijuana-growrooms/
http://www.growersguidetocannabis.com/ventilation-getting-good-air-flow-for-your-cannabis-grow/
http://growingmarijuanatips.com/the-importance-of-ventilation-in-indoor-cannabis-growing/
https://www.royalqueenseeds.com/blog-types-of-containers-for-growing-weed-n445
http://growingmarijuanatips.com/choosing-pots-and-containers-for-marijuana-growing-in-soil/
https://www.royalqueenseeds.com/blog-growing-cannabis-plants-seeds-versus-clones-n27
https://www.cropkingseeds.com/marijuana-seeds-versus-clones-which-is-better/
https://sensiseeds.com/en/blog/top-10-cannabis-strains-indoor-growing/
https://backyardcannabis.wordpress.com/2016/02/08/seeds-vs-clones/
https://www.medicaljane.com/review/super-lemon-haze-an-energizing-strain/
https://www.leafly.com/news/cannabis-101/what-is-cannabis-ruderalis
http://herb.co/2016/08/18/cannabis-ruderalis/
http://www.growweedeasy.com/best-marijuana-strains-beginners
http://www.kindgreenbuds.com/marijuana-strains/super-lemon-haze/

http://weedfarmer.com/growing_guide/cannabis_indica_sativa.php

https://www.royalqueenseeds.com/blog-top-5-cannabis-strains-for-indoor-growing-n264

http://grow-marijuana.com/strain-reviews/ak-48

http://growingmarijuanatips.com/ak-48-strains-information-growing-ak-48-marijuana/

http://howtogrowmarijuana.com/sativa-seeds/

https://www.leafly.com/news/cannabis-101/differences-growing-sativa-indica-hybrid-strains

http://www.ilovegrowingmarijuana.com/super-lemon-haze/

http://grow-marijuana.com/strain-reviews/super-lemon-haze

http://www.cannabisruderalis.com/

http://howtogrowmarijuana.com/weed-strains/super-lemon-haze-seeds/

http://www.dutch-headshop.com/en/top-marijuana-seeds-indoors-a-156.html

http://www.growweedeasy.com/lst

http://www.growweedeasy.com/cannabis-plant-training

https://www.royalqueenseeds.com/blog-low-stress-training-n100

http://www.ilovegrowingmarijuana.com/how-to-grow-marijuana-with-low-stress-training/

http://www.spliffseeds.nl/defoliation-and-pruning-cannabis-plants-for-maximum-yields.html

http://www.growweedeasy.com/defoliation

http://www.growweedeasy.com/drying-curing

http://www.growweedeasy.com/tips-tricks-curing-cannabis

https://www.leafly.com/news/cannabis-101/drying-curing-cannabis

https://www.royalqueenseeds.com/blog-how-to-cure-your-cannabis-buds-n33

http://howtogrowmarijuana.com/harvesting-marijuana-head-body-stone/

http://www.ilovegrowingmarijuana.com/harvesting-drying-curing-indoor-marijuana-plants/

http://www.growweedeasy.com/cannabis-flowering-stage

http://www.ilovegrowingmarijuana.com/flowering-stage/

https://suzyseeds.com/cannabis-seeds/growing-your-own/flowering-phase

http://www.weedsthatplease.com/flowering.htm

https://www.theweedblog.com/how-much-light-do-outdoor-marijuana-plants-need/

http://www.ilovegrowingmarijuana.com/marijuana-outdoor-basic-light-needs/

https://www.dutch-passion.com/en/grow-info/growing-cannabis-outdoors/

https://www.how-to-marijuana.com/growing-marijuana-outdoors.html

https://www.leafly.com/news/cannabis-101/outdoor-cannabis-grows-101-everything-you-need-to-start-growing-o

http://www.ilovegrowingmarijuana.com/best-places-to-grow-marijuana-outdoors/

http://grow-marijuana.com/outdoors

Image Credits

Indoor set up for growing canabis
By Plantlady223 (Own work) [CC BY-SA 4.0
(http://creativecommons.org/licenses/by-sa/4.0)], via Wikimedia
Commons
https://upload.wikimedia.org/wikipedia/commons/1/1b/Two_hydr
oponic_cannabis_plants.jpg

Grow box
https://upload.wikimedia.org/wikipedia/commons/1/1b/Two_hydr
oponic_cannabis_plants.jpg

Metal Halide Lights (MH)
https://upload.wikimedia.org/wikipedia/commons/1/17/Metaalhali
delamp.JPG

Bend down growing cannabis plants
https://upload.wikimedia.org/wikipedia/commons/a/a2/Indoor_ca
nnabis_plants.jpg

Female cannabis plant
By Photo by Rotbuche ([1]) [Public domain], via Wikimedia
Commons
https://commons.wikimedia.org/wiki/File%3ACannabis_female.jp
g

Male cannabis plant
CC BY-SA 3.0,
https://commons.wikimedia.org/w/index.php?curid=147009

Flowering
Par r0bz — Flickr, CC BY 2.0,
https://commons.wikimedia.org/w/index.php?curid=1536257

Trichomes

By Psychonaught [Public domain], via Wikimedia Commons CC BY-SA 3.0,
https://commons.wikimedia.org/w/index.php?curid=146999

Drying cannabis

By Cannabis Training University - Own work, CC BY-SA 3.0,
https://commons.wikimedia.org/w/index.php?curid=21152723

Outdoor Growing In Pots

https://upload.wikimedia.org/wikipedia/commons/e/e4/Mullaways
_Medical_Cannabis_Research_Crop.JPG

Red spider

Grizurgbg (assumed) , CC BY-SA 3.0,
https://commons.wikimedia.org/w/index.php?curid=1035267

Drying Cannabis

http://herb.co/2016/04/09/having-trouble-drying-your-weed-then-you-need-to-see-this/

12812877R00044

Made in the USA
San Bernardino, CA
10 December 2018